MW01016929

HABITAT

Also by Sue Wheeler

Solstice on the Anacortes Ferry (Kalamalka Press)

Islands (a chapbook) (Reference West)

Slow-Moving Target (Brick Books)

Understory (a chapbook) (Leaf Press)

HABITAT

SUE WHEELER

Brick Books

Library and Archives Canada Cataloguing in Publication

Wheeler, Sue, 1942–
        Habitat / Sue Wheeler.

Poems.
ISBN 1-894078-40-3

I. Title.

PS8595.H3853H33 2005   C811'.54   C2005-900402-9

We acknowledge the support of the Canada Council for the Arts,
the Government of Canada through the Book Publishing Industry
Development Program (BPIDP), and the Ontario Arts Council for
their support of our publishing program.

 Canada Council   Conseil des Arts
for the Arts   du Canada   Canadä
                                                  ONTARIO ARTS COUNCIL
                                                  CONSEIL DES ARTS DE L'ONTARIO

The cover painting is by Alison Watt, "Fire", 8 x 10 inches, mixed
media.

The author's photograph is by Ariel Rubin.

The book is set in Bembo and Franklin Gothic Condensed.

Design and layout by Alan Siu.

Printed by Sunville Printco Inc.

Brick Books
431 Boler Road, Box 20081
London, Ontario N6K 4G6

www.brickbooks.ca

30 Years Young
Brick Books 1975–2005

for Janet Barovick and Gordon Wheeler
- sister, brother

CONTENTS

I

II

III

Understory

To walk out of the field guide
and listen. To wait
for the world to approach with its dapple and hands.
Who are you?
Dreamer On A Short String.
Big Boots Clomping Through The Underbrush.
There's an understory here, shades
of meaning, tale told by a rock
signifying everything.

To open the grammar of being seen
and let the creatures name *you*.
Lover Who Begins To Notice.
Figure Of Speech.

I

Life on the Island

The road is a slice in the forest, a pale
snake, a shoelace. From my corner the road runs
seven miles to the right, seven to the left.
We haul our two-legged hearts down the gravel
past driveways and trailers and mailbox doors flapped
shut. Past the swamp where two swans overwintered,
stashing their large grey children behind the grey
thickets. Each November the wind goes *Oooo – ooo –
ooo* and we batten and stoke and light the lamps
to get through. We've done this many times. We know
the sun will lift again to bake the lichen
on the bluffs into crunch. It will bounce its glisten
off the bay and telegraph light in ripples –
messages – to the undersides of branches.
Come sit in our shade, they whisper. Look up
and read.

Preposition

The giant fir has sloughed
a spiral of bark. A fresh scar
snakes from root to sky.
This is the way the tree
accepts the lightning:
along the lines of how it grew.

Someone has laid the table for tea.
Blue cloth, honey and milk.
The family comes in from the field,
the book, the paint-job over at the cabin.
Someone fills small cups for the children.
Us, she thinks, and *here*.
What she would say fills
her body, soaks into her bones,
or maybe comes from them, the way
sap and oxygen seep from a tree.

Bones grow...
how they grow. No more choice in them
than a tree. What arrives
meets the turns the bones have taken:
a twist, a stoop, a hairline crack.

The bones in turn turn to their work.
They cook, they cut hay.
They never stop hunting
for what the heartbone's connected to.

Tea on a cloth over the plank table
cut from a tree like the tree
the storm hit. Everything prepositioned

into connection. With, beside,
from here on out. Sweetheart,
I preposition you.

Who I Am

This is the time of year I have to hide
from friends in the eastern provinces.
They do not want to hear that the snowdrops
have already faded, or how the forsythia
shouts with a thousand yellow voices.
I know I have been guilty of this
in the past. Of displaying before them
the things their climate denies. It represents
a failure on my part to understand
what Ontario winters require:
attitude, as well as a big coat.
Once, I wrote my aunt a Look-at-me! letter
listing the foods and flowers I grew.
This was forgivable. I was young, new
to gardening, and she lived in Tennessee
where any fool with soil can bring forth
eggplant. Here is what I need to explain:
By now this is who I am. The seasons
fit. This is my church and my clock,
where crocuses rise at Valentine's
and the March full moon forsythia
houses the ghosts who have lived on this upland.
It's in my boots and these dirt-lined hands.
The purple finch opens his box of song
at the top of an alder whose pollen
dusts the yard. See me on my knees, weeding –
or is it prayer? Prayer, and a fit of sneezing.

Sing a Song of Blackbirds

So long siskin, goodbye
junco, towhee and finch.
The Gang of Eight have hijacked the feeder,
redwing louts rousting regulars from the bar.
They shovel for sunflower, splashing millet and wheat
to mice and the Golden-crowned sparrow.

The meek retire to the underbrush to wait out
their inheritance. They know
this is just a phase April's going through,
a teenager slamming doors.
                                    See him
requisition the biggest maple
with its thousand lime-green chandeliers.
Into this ballroom of bloom and promise
night comes singing,
slices of fire on its shoulders.

Truth in August

I spend each day filling the day, always
something and something else in the offing –
a feeder that trickles out more as the birds eat.
Another week this hot will close the woods
to the loggers, to the artisans cutting willow.

Finches have quit the shade for the oven of 10 a.m.,
their beaks thick to crack seed, notch in the tail
for who knows what reason – a brand of truth
that's like measuring fire hazard, needle
on the forestry board pointing to green
or yellow or red, some best guess
along the flank of possibility.

Love's like that. My love
and I never vowed to be true, we arrived
at it, we keep arriving, through task
and freeze and the risk of accidental kindling.

Truth is the scatter of moth wings
over the trail, some mass moth debacle,
as if they too had stripped off all the clothes
they could and then lost the hinge of the body,
that engine of beauty.

Are the birds trying to tell us something?
Other than *Food good, no food bad*?
Crickets are cricking out the temperature.
The breeze that rocks the feeder whispers
to the fir trees, *Nothing is extra,*
and nothing is a plan. Truth

is when the paramedics lift the heat-
struck heart and its body into the ambulance
while back at the kitchen somebody prays, *O*
core of life, O bloody one, keep pumping.

What Works

The late August garden starts to brown around the edges,
creaking up off its knees and dusting its hands,
free now to turn to questions of ripeness and decline.

If I say some days I feel like gold, I don't mean workable or rare
or even shining. I mean heavier than everything I travel with.

No one told us we'd all grow up to be orphans.

House after house we lived in, my mother matching paint
to polished cotton. Does anyone today speak of
polished cotton? You do move on. You find

what works. Gold? It flakes, and tumbles in the laughing
downstream, ready to be leafed over anything it loves.

What works is the hollyhock, matching the height of the corn,
saying height makes glory as well as food.

Visitors bask in the open arms of endless golden days.
The locals are praying for rain.

October

The weather got it right this year.
Bees went ga-ga at the apple blossom's
come-hither look. Which puts you at the top
of the ladder, the pick-and-toss. I'm down here
by the boxes, good at catching, though

they always said I threw like a girl.
By definition, I might have answered, but
they did get one thing right: I never could
reckon the moment to let go. The orchard

is where the universe went *knock-knock*
on Newton's head. Who was there
was the how and why of attraction.
Maybe I'll get beaned and find the answer
to one of the big questions, like
what to make for dinner. The giant thistle,

that terrorist, has hunkered underground.
October is the fine print, the loophole
in love. The thistle's fluff-bombs go *boom!*
boom! over the harvested field. The big owl
that eats little owls shows up to scout
the backwoods, calling, *Who? Who cooks for you?*

Cold Hands

The thin gloves fished out of last year's jacket
pocket don't seem to do the job today.
It must be the fault of my heart,
storing summer's heat, reheated by the coals
each grief has dropped. Hearth, heart, heat –
the difference a letter makes, for instance
the one this morning that said
I thought you'd want to know...
Oven mitts may be what's needed
to handle a heart in this condition.
Boxer's gloves, though I've recently quit
saying to life, *Put up yer dukes.*
When I was a child, no lady would go downtown
sans nylons, heels and gloves. I'd like to be the woman
whose sent-to-her-room daughter tossed a note
that read *I hat you.* The woman who would fold
that note into a paper airplane and scribble
the answer on a wing: *I glove you.*

Darkening

Morning. Planes drop flares
over a flat calm sea, practicing rescue.
Nights when a storm flogs the water
to egg white, tugs pull in for safety and pan
their beacons over the windbreak of East Point.

Did I say "morning"? The kettle's boiling
but dawn is an hour off. November's
made a Brigadoon of summer
and everyone looks for a night
light, some version of security.
Hours back, in the wash of a dream,
I reached out my hand and you were there.

Come daybreak, we'll scramble to haul in
firewood, pick a few leaves for a salad.
Someone is sure to mention how early they turn on
the lamps. Funny how it's news each time, this
darkening. Parachuted flares hang
like the pouches of gold the rich offered
in the old days for dispensation.
I stare at these temporary planets
and burn the toast. Later, I'll gumboot
back from the garden along the downside
of afternoon, my hands filled with sorrel and cress.
November's prayer? Give us this day,
some day.

Surface Tension

To Be Here Now
try this: walk the winter trail
with a pair of 11-year-olds whose goal is
to sip as many droplets as possible
from the tips of overhanging branches.

A delicate business —
the slightest bump
will jostle the drop
before the tongue can catch it.

This tea of needle, tincture
of twig, is a water-lens
reading the world.
Today's news:
us three, a branch, the sky.

These girls are on a cusp
I barely remember, so why
do I wish I could keep them there?
Aren't we messages written in milk?
Any child knows that milk
is a disappearing ink.

December

What dream pulled this hummingbird
over rock and sea and weather
to the one Mahonia japonica in a 5-mile radius
just coming into bloom? Maybe the same dream
that leads us to watch every day
for his flare in the pricker bush making light
of the dark and the cold.
Hope is the thing with feathers,
Emily said, from her inside perch looking out.
Another Emily might have sketched him
into a foreground, backdropped by the cedars
out past the barn. Me, I'm offered this easy metaphor.
As if I think for a minute that's why he came.
        Still –
we can't help noticing how little hope weighs,
rowing the air with its hollow bones.

Wintergreen

You're singing the mid-winter blues
when the greens crawl in to shine
from the whites of your eyes.
Moss and cedar and two kinds of fir,
hemlock, arbutus, pine, salal,
the whole show foot-lamped by ferns.

One author labelled this part of the map
Grey Washcloth Laid Over a Salad.
Maybe you wish you'd said that. Maybe
you'll find the instrument that can
wrap its hollow around the rainlight
and pour forth the greens, a song for hereabouts
that goes Sword fern, Deer fern, Licorice fern.
Here where there is no dead of winter.

II

Scissors

They've just been married. It's the Depression,
way before I'm born. He has a low-paying job
but at least he has one. Each day
somebody knocks at the door.
We couldn't give them money, they'll say years later, *but
we never turned anyone away without food.*

They're like movies you only see part of,
these family stories. This one's shot outside
framing a woman and her little boy.
She wants to work for them but they have no work.
She offers to cut the grass but they have
no mower. *What about scissors,* the woman asks.
I'll cut your lawn with scissors.

What do they do next? What did any of them
do next? Eat, starve, steal, and later tell their
milk-tall post-war children, who can't imagine.
Teach them to doubt any logic that doesn't
sling a net under everyone –
can't anyone fall? –
the bold along with the meek,
who are busy inheriting the earth as a mattress, a pillow,
source of the pigweed and sorrel they pick
for roadside soup.

Whatever Happened To

The table wobbles, the pattern
on the tablecloth makes no sense –
commas? horseshoes? birds in flight?
On the table the new dial telephone,
no "Number please" at the other
end. My father clamps the receiver
with his shoulder and sorts the mail
as he chats with the friend and good
salesman he will fire six months from now
after running into him in the bar
where the good salesman's buddy
offers a smoke and asks *Are you gay too?* –
that bar my father could have sworn,
from the doorway, was *his* kind of bar.

Depends

I cocked my thumbs and fingers
into a rectangle – frame
for a possible picture.

Across this mitred universe
a large white bird flapped lazily –
one I'd never noticed in the book.

Dropped my arms for a better look.
The tiny white fly – a speck, a dot,
a millimetre – surfed and drifted

in the sunlight – the vast, unbounded
sunlight – that poured its own point of view
into every cranny of the yard.

Paris, Texas

We were huge, my mother and I,
swollen with outdoor air and light,
filling the bright doorspace.
Mother's cousin Louise sat tiny
at the far end of the room,
sunk in the science of how to abdicate
adult life. A first lesson
in perspective, lines running
from huge us to tiny her, the whole scene
meeting in Louise's thin voice:
"Don't bring that child in here (small laugh).
She won't want to see what a scarecrow
her cousin's turned into."

The picture was side-lit yellow
but this was no painter's Amsterdam
where light finds an open window
and spends itself over the canvas. This light
could cook you, it could blind you
so the shades were down and yellow
fell among the years
of daily papers around her chair.

In her day, Louise's mother, Aunt Pet,
had given up too, and sat down –
one way to cope against that tyrant
Uncle Jack, who had scared off Louise's young
husband with his rages and driven his own
son John to drink himself into the grave.

Then when my mother passed her last years
in the same metaphorical chair –
O heart, O family! –

I had to wonder: Who picks the vanishing
point? Nature or nurture,
didn't I get it either way?

Cotton

i.

The summer we were Tom and Huck
our father bought a packet of seeds.
He wanted us to understand
the South: what cotton did to the land
and the people on it. *Takes rivers,*
he said as he turned on the hose. *Wears out the soil,*
as he sprinkled Vigoro from a bag.

Did he show us where to plant, and how
deep? We were dreaming up a river
for our raft. Who hoed and weeded
between his Sweetheart roses? We tightroped
the white board fence, one foot, one foot,
above his history lesson.

I do remember the pale saucer flowers,
the powderpuffs we twisted
from the knife-edged sepals.
Slavery, he said. *Stoop labour.*
No way could two children's fingers
ever pick that jagged seed clean.

ii.

I have been to southeastern India, seen
the flat fields, the dugouts for water,
haze in the middle distance pooling
the hems of bright saris. But

this is not a travel poster.

Andhra Pradesh looks like cotton country.
Here is the salesman, his car
tanked on promises. Here are the farmers
who could do with a little cash.
Whole villages go for it, and why
not? A cottonfield in bloom is a beautiful sight (pale
saucer flowers). Bugs beyond counting agree.

Bottles with skull and crossbones
arrive with the shipment of seed.
The farmers upend the bottles onto the grub
that tunnels the cotton's sweet heart,
that pays no mind to crossbones and moves on

to carrots and beans.
Now what to do?
In one small district, up
to their necks in debt, fifty-three farmers down
the poison themselves.
Dust blows over the dry
stalks whispering, *history, history.*

To the Father at the Beach

You're scaring me. You're scaring
my granddaughter, not to mention
the shorebirds and this boy
who won't wear shoes – your arc of terror,
your, *Why do you always?*

See how small he is. Think
how small he'll look when he leaves,
the way my son left, lifting
a pack onto his hollow bones, and I didn't
run after him, didn't notice
the sharp-eyed streets or the shadows
going, *Psst. Over here.*

Maybe your son will forgive.
Mine says he does, or rather
that forgiveness isn't called for, but
this is not about guilt. Haven't you heard
the bear and cougar stories
they're swapping back in the village?
Let's keep ourselves on the upland side
of these children. Whatever lurks in the forest
will have to deal with us first.

III

The Uses of Flowers

DO YOU LIKE BUTTER?

The yellow petal
a child holds under your chin
is a test.
Pass/fail depends on the light.
The question is,
do you applaud
the gifts of this world, do you
marvel at transfiguration,
sunbeam to grass to
branching blood and so on?
Have you thanked the cows?

LOVES ME, LOVES ME NOT

Asked to solve the oldest riddle,
the daisy is no sphinx.
She splays her petals like an open book,
the pages nicked for easy ripping.

You stand at the courtroom
of someone else's heart, plucking
logic, either/or in crayon colours,
a child's drawing of the sun
before the dawn of maybe.

No ifs ands or buts, the daisy
is hooked on opposites, a Stone Age
Marxist at the bud-stage of language.
Not yet Groucho with his reel of puns
or Harpo who only honks and grins.

THE PRIMROSE PATH

Barely a sneeze past Solstice and they're up,
hot pink buds from clumps of leaves
pushy as backstage moms. Rise,
they say to their darlings,
above this ice and snow.
Gaze at the sky with your one little eye.
What do they spy?
A cloudscape of grey on grey
plus this human face, wreathed in breath.

Hear them humming, against all common sense:
Open up your overcoat!
Just forget your hat!
Let's call them jaunty, not prim.
Call them Betty, bright-eyed starlet from a 40s flick
waving her heart out at the troopship.
The camera pans the ocean
of wives, mothers, girlfriends.
Betty's perfume, all shoulder pads and dark lipstick,
is the scent of a picked blossom
that pans your synapse map as only a smell can
and lifts you past the socked-in garden till suddenly
you're flopped in a flowering meadow
one long-lost summer afternoon.

January, that black and white documentary
on the subject of Play now, pay later,
grabs you by the elbow, muttering something
about being led down the famous path,
about hard frosts in the offing
and Don't say I didn't warn you.

Meanwhile, primroses polka-dot winter
with promise.
That the soldier will come back.
That Betty will wait and the meadow,
surely, green again. Meanwhile,
sheep have moseyed through the left-open gate
and are headed straight for the flowerbed.

IN THE MATTER OF ROSES,

be grateful so little was promised.
The gardener walks out
with her basket of tools.
She snips the finished flowers
to keep the plant in bloom.
Deadheading.

Deadhead also means
a log so soaked it hangs
at the water's face, waiting
to bite your boat. Safety
was never promised either
though you did get eyes,
a tiller, and a floater coat.

This gratitude will free you
to welcome whatever opens,
then shuts around the cold-struck
bee at night. To celebrate
the near-misses.
The War of Roses.
Thorns.

IV

On the Water

bones hunger home – Gary Snyder

FEBRUARY

Sometimes, in the middle of a dark wood,
something lights the way. At 6 a.m.
the path to the outhouse shines with overnight snow.
The kids will be beside themselves.
Beside snow angels and men with carrot noses.

Other times, the dark way takes the two little girls
who've rowed out through the Narrows to the store boat, 1923.
They've brought the leather bucket for the ice cream
and for one last lesson on the tide and its rapids.

This morning the branches of East Point
broadcast angel music, the warble and chirp of two eagles
back from Squamish or Qualicum,
fat on spawned-out salmon.
First the fish, then the birds, headed for the nest.
When you migrate, there's no place like home.

MARCH

The flurry out the window isn't snow, it's
a scatter of fir scraps, siskins and chickadees
stripping the cones of seed.
Eat one drop one,
onto the bed of last year's seedlings
in a program to flummox the question
Where or which is the habitat?
Tiny claws hang on for dear life to the branches.
The branches reach into acres of passing wings.

Dear Life,
I am writing to ask that you not confuse us
with easy answers. Please keep sending
days like this, days we can't see the forest
for the birds. Their buzz-buzz-chatter
is the same old tune:
sex and territory, love and home.
Thank you for playing our song.

BACK IN DECEMBER

The wind blew so hard that night the light bent,
plate glass a flexing belly dance of reflected room.
The roof joined the performance, shedding
a swath of shingles we'd be finding for weeks in the woods,
here, then there, the way bad news
dawns gradually. Fir and cedar toppled
in a giant's game of pick-up sticks,
blocking the way to the neighbour's house.

This estate's as real as it gets:
flooded path, leaking roof,
fenceposts with mid-life bad knees.
Have you noticed how things go first
at the interface? –
            post with ground, house with sky –
as if they, too, struggled with relationship.
Minus us, the place would relax
to blackberry, alder, the fir inchlings
I pull out of each spring's pea patch.
A born-again forest primeval on its way to birdland,
the sky-fall of next century's windstorms.

Back in September a friend left the Trade Center lobby,
no more roof or else
nothing but roof
and then more roof
over him,
jet fuel
falling around him,
and walked north until he found
a working pay phone for the only message
anyone wanted to hear:
I'm OK.

APRIL

The grey sky opens for a minute, then closes.
Blink of a blue-eyed god.
The buzz of a chainsaw says
my dark-eyed love is cutting the winter's blow-down
to heat the little cube we've borrowed
from space. What does the world want
as interest?
Interest?

Daffodils slowly paint the verges yellow,
thumbprints of Eva Tucker, homesteading the 20s and 30s.
Her bluebells run in right angles, cabin
sunk to the sketch somebody made by lamplight
back in Alberta, relocating their loves and their losses,
the dream of owning land out west.

The songbirds are back from winter vacation
right on schedule – Warblers March 23rd,
Goldfinch the first of May –
time's apparent pattern we slip into
easy as a sleeve
and then find the ace:
one heart, no blueprint.

MAY

An ordinary woman
inches along the garden path, weeding carrots.
After the season's fifth funeral she shivers
when she pulls this hard at what she cannot see.

A little man might pop up from the root zone
to grant a wish, any wish, for his recent liberation.
(Maybe those fools in the stories
are only the ones you hear about.
Maybe she'd be tempted.
Like the birds and the trees
she can use all the help she can get.
Griefs piling up like cordwood.
The tiny slow fire beneath her heart.)

A breeze at her cheek whispers
news of the friends who are on the water,
paddling Jervis Inlet
against the current and the outflow wind.
The old-timers did this from need:
row the cream and eggs twenty miles to the float camp,
row to French Creek for the mail.

Home is where someone
held this same invisible stern-line,
a spider with her spinnerets, and
is that a southeaster picking up?
Each day she could call Mayday! Mayday!
and not be crying wolf.

V

Tideflat Suite

TITLE

The moon at noon has pulled the oceans up
like old-fashioned skirts for the rock-
to-rock fording of a stream.
Which gives the woman a bay
to walk across, wondering, Is the bay

the water, or the bowl that holds it?
For decades weeds and gills here choked
on the bark and forest soil from shipped-out logs.
Now at least the eelgrass is creeping back
and flatfish skim past swimmers' legs.

The sun thunders in.
Nothing old-fashioned in the way
people duck for shade and coat their children
in promising lotions. No one ever promised her
any kind of garden, but she knows

it wasn't supposed to be like this.
Back when the frogs were OK.
Back when plants ate just enough light,
and the bay had title to itself.

THE TIDE

doesn't wait for a woman,
either. She can daydream, lose the thread,
forget the date for planting potatoes, and still
there's this clockwork down at the bay.

She rubs the dough off her hands
and heads to the water-meadow,
eelgrass drawn by the sucked-out sea,
a thousand green compass needles, pointing.

December, it's dark when the water's out
but today is June: sun heats
the pavement of clamshell and pools
a tiny shadow at her feet. Her step
on the mudflat sends the shy heron
flapping and *gronk*ing over the headland.

Did she think she could walk here
with no disturbance? Winter or summer
her passage is black or blue,
her bootprint soaked in sky.

WEEDS

Let's hear it for the Glaucous-winged Gull,
pale philosopher of *eat-what-falls*,
common as dirt, our mothers would say.
Let's hear it for the alders
who uncleared the clearing
the minute our backs were turned.
Next island over, a whole preserve
surrounds an acre of lilies.
This is as it should be.
The lily, and much else, needs help, the lily
and the river, where once-upon-a-time
salmon thronged so numberless
they cobbled the waters to a coppery street.

I've seen a frog caught in a snake's jaws.
The frog cried out, but no help came.
I can't say how it goes with snakes and frogs.
But think of the way the gulls replied
when an eagle taloned one in the neck.
The eagle had barely lifted her prize
before the storm of wings and screaming
harried her off.
            Think how alders reach
to cover the cut-over ground. And how
they used to call the black coats *weeds* –
the ones widows wore
when they took up their stations of grief.

THAT'S THE WAY

The way the
Great Blue Heron
distills the grey
of the shallows
that lie receptive
to the sky's mood.

The way
the heron takes
all that
into beak and feather
and tracks the message
from fish to eye
to mind to muscle to

fish!

and comes up flinging
scraps of light
off the silver dart
it now opens to
and gulps down whole.

That Summer Ma Pickled Everything

The spring of my sixtieth year
a lot of things start to give out.

Maybe you're thinking *eyes? hips?*
memory? What I mean is
the camera, the computer, the pressure
canner and two roofs –
solid, themselves, not metaphors.

The camera, canner and roofs lasted
twenty-five years. A friend writes me a birthday poem
asking
            Who lived all this life?

One summer I tried to pickle everything –
the children on the swings,
the smell of 5 a.m. out on the water,
a rainbow that hung around for an hour,
casting its double onto the western sea. Friends
flitted through like butterflies, lit, settled, sipped,
moved on.

A term deposit has turned into stuff.
Camera, computer, canner.
Let's call each roof a crest, capital, cover.
Cappuccino, the way they rise to the ridge cap,
take a small breath and
rise again, peak on the hood of a Capuchin monk.
Two pale metal roofs the colour of coffee
spooned into milk, set to watch the next quarter century
pass like air out of a perfect cowl of foam.

Canary: A Dream

We loved our house beside the river.
No rugs, no pictures, and who needed tables
or chairs? Low windows welcomed the riverlight.
My son, cradling his baby, stooped to look out
at the lawn filling with townspeople
dressed in carnival colours. He looked
at the water driven by a downriver wind
and the shack built smack against the dam.
"Canary" we called that shack, the first thing
that would go. Whipped water licked
over the levee, a tease, like beer-foam on TV.
I hurried from room to room, shaking
the children sacked out on bare mattresses.
No dice! Those kids would sleep through anything.
I wish I could say the water turned and dropped.
Pushed by dream-physics, it rose
from every direction. If only I could tell you
those splendid people noticed in time.
A woman danced barefoot on the grass,
arms wide, her throat to the sky, singing
the title tune from the latest musical, a smash hit.

Notions

The sewing machine hums
its little start-up hum, stitching
up the britches you've had so long
they're old enough to drink and vote.
Those camel-coloured cords
have a rip, a tear, and your tear
shed for the passing of all things.
The tear shed is where you stack
your sorrows, cordwood
for another winter's downside.

If life is a fabric store, you
are up against the wall of notions
wondering, Should I trust the bias
binding? You'll never get out
alive. Each four-eyed button's
in a staring contest with two
thousand overhead watts.
The needles whisper *uh-oh*
as a herd of camels noses in,
cocky as a passel of rich men.

One hump or two?
The notions you come up with
will be your come-down.
In other words your comeuppance.
To check your I.D.
you stand before a mirror.
After you, says the mirror
and shows you the door.

Present

Time was a fiction, somebody said, place
was the earth's hot romance.
We were kids, we didn't know
Einstein had folded Here into Now
like egg white into batter, but
we were figuring this out for ourselves.
Didn't we answer *present*
when the teacher called the roll?
What we meant was *here*.
The flip side was *now*, pinning
the dates on pyramids and battles.

Which left Robbie Hill studying Before,
when he'd had a mother, and Forever,
when he wouldn't. He considered the one
hand, and the other, until past and future
collapsed into an endless present, a new given
he couldn't find a word for,
and those hands lit a fire
under the only historic building in the city park.

The park was a trove of arrowheads.
We pictured the Ancients,
who would have taken better notice
of a boy's grief, hunting and gathering
while the earth cooled, dreaming up
language and barbecue.
They were old pros at space-time,
drumming up music and fire
for death and every other passage
to keep the heavens turning.

ই

When I say you've moved the earth for me
I don't mean just the garden
or all those ditches.
It's your birthday. We gather
like the motherless children we are,
or sometimes feel.
Like the Ancients, with feast and drink.
Here now,
isn't that worth a present,
isn't that worth a song? –
plus this bright idea: as many words as we can eat,
heaped with roses and sugar,
sporting their own tiny bonfire.

Monarchs

Then there was that time in California,
Monarchs dotting the eucalyptus,
coming or going, I forget, along their map
that survives the meltdown of metamorphosis,
survives being wormy and later being beautiful.

That was the night the storm erased the highway
and the toasters, leaving us cold cuts around the candles
and talk of home, the one we suddenly couldn't get to.
We took our homebodies to bed as the ocean
relieved the cliff of the next few inches of underburden,
bringing the beds that much closer to the beach.

Dawn revealed a black-and-gold Jackson Pollock,
a crazy-quilt of smashed and sundered wings.
Someday the handful we picked up and lost track of
will ghost into a woman's lap as she opens
the paperback novel. The one that deals with
dark happenings to gold-plated real estate.
Story of what's in store for the delicate,
no matter how astonishing their code.

VI

The Next Day

So little separates the quick
from the recently dead. It's as if
the glass wall at the far end of Customs
were no longer frosted, and we could see them
clear as yesterday, and they could see us.
Surely they'd want to see us. They
look back. The simplest things have turned
mysterious. They study the marks
on the glass doors. TUO.
TUO? They look at each other.
They shrug and shake their heads.
It must be language, but it's written
in a code they will never, ever, decipher.

God

And what if there is, after all,
a god? What if it walks among us
touching each one lightly
on the shoulder? Asking,
Where is your life?
This god, would it be the flower, or the flower's
opening, or the space the flower opens into?
How about the wind, arriving as you pitch
the tent, or later, wind keeping mosquitoes away?
Maybe it's copper, Earth's arteries, dug
and hammered and traded, fingered and pocketed
at every market in the world.
The man in the blue scarf offers
three pieces of god for a hank of wool.
The coin passes. It whispers, *As you were.*

Humans

As if we're put on earth to forget the ending.

— Larry Levis

It's the old thought, isn't it? —
how coffee goes on being offered,
and menus collected, each night
rewinding us to the place
of mild expectancy, just inside
the restaurant door.

Here is what I love about humans:
that slightly pleasant, slightly
dumb expression on our faces,
eyes not quite adjusted from
the sidewalk light. The tiny
lift of the chin that asks if
there's a table by the window.

Hope

And then, after everything, and in spite
of what we know, hope offers its hand.
The hand travels the furrow, dropping
seed into April soil, conjuring green
from apparent nothing. Soup from a stone.

Take this basket somebody wove out of air
and willow. My great-grandfather used it
for picking berries. As a youth he'd seen
brother killing brother at Gettysburg.
Blood down the wagon tracks. There's the basket
on the old man's arm as he pokes along
the river, August, 1910. Bee-song
tossing the later blossoms. His hand reaches
up, toward the branches bent with sugar.

Italian

After a supper of red beans and rice that glistened,
  each grain,
    each fat bean,
      in the lamplight;

after we've washed the flowered plates and stood them upright in the rack;

after twenty-one years during which
  cars kept to their half of the road
    illness halted just inside the door
      and lightning took its business elsewhere –

we have this one winter night.

Let's be Italian.
  Let's clink glasses on the piazza beside the ticking stove.
    Tell me more about yourself.
      Talk with your hands.

Winter Solstice

To carry yourself forward and experience myraid things is an illusion.
But myriad things coming forth and experiencing themselves is awakening.

— Dogen

The other day a sheep spent three hours at the bottom of a cliff
waiting for the tide to turn and offer some beach to walk on.
The water came forth, and the wind,
and the stone bluff, unforgiving in lilac and ochre,
fissuring down to the sea.
The moss, the sheep,
the day, for that matter, dim and cold, came forth.
Time, too, was a player in this scene.
We meant to watch to see how it worked out, but friends
dropped by, and distractions.

Solstice. The sun stands.
To us it feels like it's the dark
that does the standing, now before it turns
to head south.
That familiar sky line across the bay — silhouette of tall tree,
dead tree, tree with a broken top where eagles perch.
The rock's knowledge of rock
may be everything, and enough.
And anyway, nothing about the sky is a line.
To say clouds part is cliché.
In the low grey ceiling, a little cloud-mouth
opens and says *blue*, says *morning*, says
Over here!

NOTES

"Understory": Ideas for this poem came from the writings of Don McKay and from Stephanie Strickland's "WaveSon.net 12," in *V* (Penguin, 2002).

"On the Water": "bones hunger home" is from Gary Snyder's "Old Bones," in *Mountains and Rivers Without End* (Counterpoint, 1996).

"Wintergreen": The notion of Cascadia's winter climate being a grey washcloth laid over a salad is found in Tom Robbins's *Another Roadside Attraction* (Ballantine, 1972).

"That Summer Ma Pickled Everything": This poem is for Tony, Bruce, Paddy, and Colin, roofers supreme. The title comes from a print, "Ma Pickled Everything Last Summer," by Sidney Roark, which shows pantry shelves holding jars filled with birdsong, watermelon, lightning, a sailboat, etc.

"Humans": The epigraph is a line from Larry Levis's poem "Elegy for Whatever Had a Pattern in It," in *Elegy* (University of Pittsburgh Press, 1997).

"Winter Solstice": the statement from the Zen philosopher Dogen is quoted in many works on him and his sayings.

ACKNOWLEDGMENTS

Thanks:
To Liz Phillips, who edited the manuscript with incisiveness and respect.
To the Nanaimo Women Poets for the fine companionship and critiques.
To my family and friends and the Lasqueti Island community, for the time and the continued encouragement.
Special thanks to my partner Peter Johnston.

Some of the poems were previously published in the chapbook *Understory* (Leaf Press), in *The Malahat Review, Event, Grain, The Fiddlehead, The Cream City Review, The New Quarterly*, and in the anthologies *Vintage 2000* (League of Canadian Poets), *Is This Forever, or What?* (Greenwillow Books), *From the Basement* (Leaf Press), and *The Invention of Birds* (Leaf Press). "Understory" appeared on the website Poetry Daily (www.poems.com). "Italian" has been translated into Spanish and published in the journal *Posdata*.

My gratitude to the editors.

Sue Wheeler is the author of two previous books of poetry. Her first book *Solstice on the Anacortes Ferry* (Kalamalka Press) was shortlisted for both the Pat Lowther and the Gerald Lampert Awards. *Slow-Moving Target* (Brick Books) was shortlisted for the 2001 Pat Lowther Award and the 2001 BC Book Prize for Poetry. Sue Wheeler lives and works on a farm on Lasqueti Island, BC.